© 2006 Gerald Singer
Printed in China by Everbest Printing Company Ltd.
ISBN 0-9641220-6-5
Library of Congress Control Number 2005905511

Written by Gerald Singer
Photographs by Don Hebert, Dean Hulse, Steve Simonsen & Gerald Singer
Front Cover Photograph by Steve Simonsen
Back Cover Photograph by Habiba Hussein
Edited by Habiba Hussein
Graphic Design by Elisa Bryan

Sombrero Publishing Company
P.O. Box 1031
St. John, US Virgin Islands 00831
Website: www.StJohnBeachGuide.com

Photo by Gerald Singer

"... out to the windy beach,
Far from the twisted reach
of crazy sorrow..."

Bob Dylan,
"Hey Mr. Tambourine Man"

Photo by Steve Simonsen

St. John Beach Guide
Table of Contents

What's So Special About St. John Beaches?

The sand is soft, powdery and sensual. It extends into the sea so that you can wade into the water easily, safely and comfortably.

The water is just the right temperature, refreshing, but not cold. It's crystal-clear and calm, possessing a wide assortment of colors ranging from light turquoise, to green and dark blue, offset by the reds and oranges of the nearby coral reefs.

The beaches lie within small, protected bays, surrounded by green hills and bordered by shade providing, tropical vegetation, such as coconut palms, seagrapes and beach mahos.

The views are spectacular. From just about every beach, you'll enjoy a panorama of islands, cays, rocks and small bays.

In addition to all this, most of St. John beaches are protected by the Virgin Islands National Park and remain natural and undeveloped.

Last but not least, St. John beaches are located on St. John, United States Virgin Islands, truly an American paradise.

Photo by Steve Simonsen

Introduction

The saying, "one picture is worth a thousand words," is especially true for St. John beaches. It is for this reason that I have relied more heavily on photographs than the proverbial thousand words to describe each beach.

This guide covers 15 of the most accessible, white sand beaches located within the National Park. It is designed for short-term visitors, those staying a few hours or a few weeks, who want to make the most of their time here. The goal is to help answer the frequently-asked question, *"which beach should I go to today?"*

Acknowledgements

The making and evolution of this book was a team effort and I would like to express my appreciation to some of the most important team members.

To my beautiful partner and editor, Habiba, who provided her artistic input, attention to detail and much-needed moral support.

To the photographers Don Hebert, Dean Hulse and Steve Simonsen who have succeeded in capturing the magnificent beauty of St. John beaches.

And to our graphic designer, Elisa Bryan, who put it all together.

Beach Ecology

Where Does the Sand Come From?

St. John's beach sand comes, almost entirely, from the coral reef community. This is the main reason why our sand is so much finer and softer then the sand found on most continental beaches, which comes from terrestrial sources, such as the weathering of rocks.

Most of our sand is produced by the force of waves and currents acting on the coral reef as coral, calcareous algae, (algae with a hard exoskeleton) the shells of various sea creatures and sea urchin spines (which make up those little black grains of sand) are gradually broken down into sand-sized grains.

In addition, reef grazing fish, such as parrotfish (photo on right), produce a significant amount of the sand found on our beaches. Parrotfish exist on a diet of algae, which they scrape off the surface of coral with fused teeth, which look like a parrot's beak. They then grind this coral and algae mixture to a fine powder. The algae covering the coral are absorbed as food. The remainder of their meal passes through their digestive tracts and is excreted in the form of sand.

Parrotfish are not shy, and by donning a mask, a pair of fins and a snorkel, you can observe them at work and even hear the sound of their beaks scraping against the coral. Every so often you may witness them relieving themselves of the indigestible portions of their meal in the form of a fine sand that will settle slowly to the bottom of the reef. Other grazing fish, such as the blue tang, perform the same function. The amount of sand produced in this manner is considerable - about one ton of sand per acre of reef per year.

How Does the Sand Get to the Beach?

Sand is basically a waste product of the coral reef. This waste, which would otherwise suffocate the coral, is removed by the action of waves and currents over the reef. This sand collects in a kind of storage area around the perimeter of the reef.

During the winter, large ocean swells are generated by storms and cold fronts coming from North America and from over the central Atlantic. When these reach the north shore of St. John, they become steeper and break on the shore. This winter phenomenon is called ground sea and it serves to move the sand from the storage areas around the reef depositing it on the beach.

In the summer the same process can occur on the southern coasts, caused by the action of the trade winds or tropical storms.

How Is Sand Lost From Beaches?

Although sand is regularly brought to the beach from the sea, it is also consistently being lost from the beach. Because most St. John beaches are found within bays protected by headlands, or points, on both sides of the beach, sand is not washed laterally along the coast and lost in this manner, as is the case on the beaches of the continental United States.

However, sand from the drier upper portion of the beach is often blown by winds past the line of vegetation where it will stay forever in the form of soil.

On the wetter lower beach, sand is constantly washed back and forth by waves. This makes the grains get smaller and smaller. When they get so fine that they go into suspension, they are washed back out to sea and lost.

Hurricanes or strong tropical storms are other natural phenomena that could result in sand loss. Large storms may either take away or add sand to existing beaches. They may even create new beaches. In general, extremely high ground seas and hurricanes accompanied by high tides will send large amounts of sand past the vegetation line or wash it back out to sea so far that the depth of the water will be too deep for the sand to be recycled by ordinary ground seas. Moreover, these storms often destroy large sections of reef, reducing the sand supply for years to come.

The Balance

The lost sand will be replaced by the reef community and the beaches will remain in their sandy state. That is, as long as the dynamics of sand production and sand loss are in balance. This balance can be disturbed by natural causes such as hurricanes or coral diseases or as a result of interferences by human beings in the natural order of nature. These interferences can be continual and permanent creating more insidious imbalances, than the imbalances caused by natural factors.

Removing sand from the beach or the sea floor can have extremely long lasting effects. For example, dredging operations often take sand from sand storage areas, preventing new sand from reaching the beaches in times of ground seas or tropical storms.

Removing sand from the beach can also result in irreversible sand loss. When St. John first began to experience the boom in tourism with the resultant construction of roads and buildings, a great deal of sand was taken from the beaches to make concrete. The loss of sand in this manner was so dramatic that several beaches never recovered and are now considerably narrower than they used to be. (For instance the now relatively narrow Big Maho Bay used to be one of the widest beaches on St. John.) The process of recovery from this interference is extremely slow, and if the dredging or the mining of sand is continual, the sand beach will be replaced by rocky shoreline.

The worst threat to beaches comes from damage to the coral reef.

It is important to remember that a healthy coral reef is responsible for the continued existence of our beaches, and those factors that negatively impact the reef, such as pollution or runoff caused by irresponsible development will eventually lead to the disappearance of perhaps St. John's most valuable resource, its beaches.

Photo by Don Hebert

Snorkeling Dangers and Environmental Concerns

Many beginning snorkelers are uncomfortable in the water because they are afraid of what unknown terrors may be lurking about. Most of these fears, especially the fear of fish, are either unreasonable or grossly exaggerated. On the other hand, there are other, more probable, dangers that the beginning snorkeler may not even be aware of.

Sharks

The most common fear is the fear of sharks, a preoccupation that has become almost a national obsession, due mostly to movies like "Jaws." Nonetheless, if you are snorkeling in the Virgin Islands in relatively shallow water, near the shore, and are not spear fishing, chances are great that you will never even see a shark. On the unlikely event that you do see one, it is extremely doubtful that it will have the slightest interest in you. For extra safety, calmly snorkel back to the beach or your boat.

Barracudas

The next most feared fish is the barracuda. They are curious and often come alongside a snorkeler and look at them. Barracudas have the disconcerting habit of opening and closing their mouths displaying their sharp teeth and a serious overbite. This motion is not meant to frighten or to warn. It is simply a part of the way they breathe. Barracudas feed on fish very much smaller than themselves, which would exclude big, fierce-looking human beings.

I have never known of anyone getting attacked by a barracuda, and this includes spearfishers and SCUBA divers. But, to stay on the safe side, it would probably be better not to wear shiny jewelry while snorkeling. The theory here is that a visually challenged barracuda or one hunting in murky water might mistake that glittering object for a little fish and go after it. I've never known of this actually happening, but it won't hurt to take this precaution.

Although anything is possible, not everything is probable. Shark and barracuda attacks on Virgin Island snorkelers are so overwhelmingly improbable that they should not be a cause for concern.

Photo by Dean Hulse

13

Jellyfish

Another animal to watch out for is the jellyfish. Most species encountered in the Virgin Islands, such as the commonly found moon jelly, (photo on right) are fairly innocuous and contact with their tentacles usually has no effect at all. People with sensitive skin, however, could get a mild rash.

A more dangerous jellyfish, the sea wasp or box jelly, also can be found in our waters, but far less frequently. They are translucent with a dome-shaped body about three inches long and have four tentacles about six to twelve inches long. Although some people can have a serious allergic reaction, usually the sting, which is not nearly as bad as a regular wasp sting, leaves you with an itchy welt that takes about a week to go away. Treat sea wasp stings by applying vinegar over the effected area.

Photo by Dean Hulse

Corals

Snorkelers should be aware that there are other dangerous animals that they do need to watch out for. First and foremost are corals. Yes, corals are animals, not plants or rocks, although they do have a rock-like exoskeleton that is sharp and coarse. When your skin is wet, it can be cut easily and even light contact against coral may result in abrasions that can be itchy, annoying, and slow to heal.

Not only can coral hurt you, but also you can hurt it. Just lightly brushing up against live coral can damage the surface mucus layer, making the animal more susceptible to infection. Worse yet, is when snorkelers inadvertently kick coral with their fins or actually stand on the living coral reef when they get tired or frightened. Coral is extremely slow growing, so the results of such damage can be long lasting.

Sea Urchin

The spiny sea urchin also presents a potential danger to snorkelers. These are the black spherical creatures that look like little black land mines. The central body is about two to three inches in diameter and the spines can be as long as eight inches. If you step on or bump into one, the sharp spines can easily puncture your skin, break off and remain imbedded there. Once in your flesh, the spines are difficult to get out. They usually dissolve after a while, but the wounds can be painful and annoying.

The key to dealing with sea urchins is to avoid them. If you are getting into the water at a rocky or coral strewn location, wear your fins into the water. Walk backwards and watch where you step. When snorkeling, watch where you're going, especially in shallow water or in tight quarters within the reef.

The Most Dangerous Creature of All

Another extremely dangerous creature often found in Virgin Island waters is the human being driving a motor boat, so be on the lookout. If snorkeling in areas not protected by swim buoys, use a dive flag and be especially careful.

Know Your Limits

An additional aspect of snorkeling safety is to be aware of the water conditions and to recognize your own limitations. These will change with time and location, so take into consideration factors such as wind, waves, currents, breaking surf, boat traffic, water clarity and depth as well as your experience level and physical condition. Stay within your comfort zone and use a floatation device if necessary.

Don Hebert

Don has been photographing the Caribbean islands for more than twenty four years and has established himself as one of the leading photographers in the Virgin Islands. His work has been on the covers of more than 100 publications. Some of the most noteworthy are: Travel & Leisure, Caribbean Travel & Life, Eastern Airlines, Midway Airlines and Hollywood Reporter–as well as many local publications.

Don was named in the list of top ten photographers to shoot in the Caribbean by Caribbean Travel & Life magazine. In addition to the many local publications featuring his work, he has been published in Islands magazine, Vogue, Coastal Living, Caribbean Travel & Life, Island Home, and Cruising World. His stock photos have appeared in quite a number of international ad campaigns, and Don has shot for the U.S. Virgin Islands, Grenada and St. Kitts & Nevis' ad campaigns.

Don lives on St. Thomas with his wife Erica and children Stephen and Kendall. Visit him at www.donhebert.com, e-mail: don@donhebert.com or phone: 340-777-6484

Dean Hulse

Dean is a retired St. John public school teacher. As well as being an excellent photographer, Dean is an avid scuba diver, sharpshooter and all–around adventurer. He currently winters on St. John and summers in Parachute, Colorado where he photographs and participates in the fast–growing sport, Cowboy Action Shooting.

Steve Simonsen

I was first introduced to Steve Simonsen's photography when a friend literally dragged me to see a slide show that was being presented at the Cinnamon Bay Campground. I resisted because to me, the term "slide show" conjured up memories of an evening spent viewing slides of a family function or a trip to Europe – "There's Uncle Al and that's the Eiffel Tower".

Well, Steve and his wife Janet had put together a slide show that wasn't like that at all. Everyone in attendance at the outdoor amphitheater sat spellbound, transfixed by the cascade of powerful images and the well-chosen music that accompanied them. After the presentation, I looked around at the audience – there wasn't a dry eye to be seen.

Steve's work has been featured in prestigious magazines such as Caribbean Travel & Life, Islands, Playboy's Sexy Swimsuits, and National Geographic Traveler. Recently, Steve has published Living Art, a photographic study of the natural beauty of St. John. For more information visit www.stevesimonsen.com.

Gerald Singer

Gerald Singer, "the World's Foremost Authority on St. John Beaches," lives on St. John with his wife, Habiba and their son Jacob. Regarding the numerous and repeated visits to the beaches necessitated in compiling the information for this book, Gerald admits, "it's a tough job, but someone has to do it."

North Shore Beaches

Francis Bay
Maho Bay
Cinnamon Bay
Trunk Bay
Hawksnest Bay
Caneel Bay
Honeymoon Bay
Salomon Bay

Photo by Steve Simonsen

South Shore Beaches

Lameshur Bay

Great Lameshur Bay

Grootpan Bay

Kiddle Bay

Salt Pond Bay

Photo by Steve Simonsen

There are two beautiful and easily accessible National Park beaches on the south shore of St. John, Salt Pond and Lameshur Bays. Both are comparable to the north shore beaches and are free from the breaking waves that effect the north shore when cold fronts arrive during the winter months.

Photo by Steve Simonsen

Why Salomon Bay?

There is no road to the beach at Salomon Bay. To get there, you'll need to take a trail or arrive by boat.

Although Salomon is every bit as beautiful as any of St. John's incomparable north shore beaches, this unconventional access, keeps the number of visitors down and insures a more intimate beach experience. Additionally, if you've come by ferry from St. Thomas for the day or are staying in Cruz Bay, you won't need to rent a car or hire a taxi to get to the beach.

How to Get There

Take the Lind Point Trail, which begins at the National Park Visitors Center in Cruz Bay. It is a little less than one mile to the beach at Salomon Bay. When you reach to the fork in the trail you can go either way. The lower trail is slightly shorter and less hilly. On the other hand, the upper trail is more scenic, passing by the beautiful Lind Point Overlook, with its magnificent view of Cruz Bay Harbor.

From either the upper or lower trails, take the spur trail to Salomon Bay, which will be on your left and leads downhill.

For a shorter walk (a little over a half mile, all down hill, but all uphill on the way back) to Salomon Beach, take the North Shore Road (Route 20) past Mongoose Junction and up the hill. Turn left at the top of the hill where there is a blue Virgin Islands National Park sign.

Immediately on the right hand side is a parking area for approximately four vehicles. Park here if you drove. The Caneel Hill Spur Trail intersects Route 20 and is clearly marked with a sign.

Take this trail north and downhill to the Lind Point Trail and turn left. Then take the first spur trail to the right, which goes down the hill to Salomon Bay.

Proper Attire

Because of its long-standing reputation of being a clothing optional beach, it is common to find sunbathers at Salomon Bay with no attire at all.

Nonetheless, would-be nudists should be advised that park rangers have been enforcing Virgin Islands anti-nudity laws and issuing citations to non-compliers.

For now, those who might be offended by nudity can sidestep this issue by choosing the close-by Honeymoon Beach as an alternative destination.

Facilities

There are no facilities at Salomon Bay.

Photo by Steve Simonsen

23

Snorkeling

Some of the finest snorkeling on the north shore can be found in the area of the fringing reef that lies around the point separating Salomon and Honeymoon Bays on the northeast corner of Salomon beach. Most of the reef lies in calm, shallow water with some sections even rising above the surface at times of extreme low tides. Thus, snorkelers should make an extra effort to avoid situations where the water is too shallow for them.

The coral reef here supports a diverse marine community. The coral is colorful, the fish are plentiful and there is a great deal to see and enjoy.

This is the most easily accessible near-shore snorkel in St. John, and it can be thoroughly enjoyed by snorkelers of all experience levels.

Snorkel in areas protected by swim buoys to minimize danger from boat traffic in the area.

Snorkeling just off the beach is a good way for beginners to get practice before attempting to snorkel over the reef.

Photo by Steve Simonsen

Honeymoon Bay

Why Honeymoon Bay?

Honeymoon and Salomon Beaches are separated by a small rocky point of land. They both contain the magnificent qualities common to all the beaches of St. John's north shore, but they differ from the other beaches primarily in how you get there. You can go by boat, but almost everyone arrives by trail.

Walking along these forest paths gives you the chance to experience the beauty and tranquility of the unspoiled interior of St. John. Although the hike is relatively easy, there is enough of a physical challenge to make your arrival at the beach, followed by a cooling dip in the crystal-clear Caribbean, a sensuous and welcome reward.

Consequently, if you like the idea of taking a trail to the beach or if you want to experience the excellent snorkeling described for Salomon Beach, Honeymoon Beach is a fine alternative. It lies just to the east of Salomon and enjoys the same natural beauty and fantastic views. The snorkeling reef fringes the rocky point between the two bays and is just as easily accessible from either beach.

Getting There

Like Salomon there is no road to Honeymoon. You need to walk the trail or go by boat.

Shortest Walk

For the shortest , but steepest walk (less than a half mile, with a descent of 250 feet) to Honeymoon Beach, take Route 20 past Mongoose Junction and up the hill. Turn left at the top of the hill where there is a blue Virgin Islands National Park sign.

Immediately on the right hand side is a parking area for approximately four vehicles. From here you will see the sign for the Lind Point Trail that leads to the beach.

Easiest Walk

The Caneel Bay Resort provides public land access to Caneel and Honeymoon Beaches. Unlike the narrow forest trail that winds down a rocky hillside, the dirt road from the Caneel Bay parking lot is well-maintained and there are no hills to climb. On your way to the beach, you can enjoy the magnificent landscaping that borders the road.

From Town

If you would rather walk from town, Honeymoon can also be reached by taking the Lind Point Trail. It will be a little over a mile from Cruz Bay to Honeymoon. Follow the directions to Solomon Bay, but when you get to the Solomon Bay spur, continue on the Lind Point Trail instead of turning left.

Facilities

Facilities available at Honeymoon include wooden picnic tables, garbage cans and an old block and wooden structure that could serve as a private changing area or to provide shelter in the advent of a sudden squall.

Shade

Honeymoon offers the possibility of shade beneath the large maho tree near the center of the beach or under one of the low-lying seagrapes.

Lind Point
Trail
→

VIRGIN ISLANDS
NATIONAL PARK

Photo by Don Hebert

Only the reef area on the west is protected by swim buoys, thus allowing boats to come right up to the rest of the beach. As the only north shore beach where this is permitted, Honeymoon Bay has become a favorite destination of day charter boats, which often arrive in late morning and depart by mid afternoon.

Photo by Don Hebert

Photo by Gerald Singer

Honeymoon Bay

Snorkeling Reef

Salomon Bay

Snorkeling

The excellent coral reef described in the Salomon Bay chapter lies off the rocky point on the west side of Honeymoon Beach.

Photo by Don Hebert

Photo by Steve Simonsen

Caneel Bay

Photo by Steve Simonsen

Why Caneel Bay?

Caneel Bay Beach is a good choice if you would like to combine a day at the beach with lunch at the Caneel Bay Resort. Take a swim, a snorkel or just relax. When you get hungry, you can enjoy a well-prepared meal at one of the hotel's seaside restaurants, the Caneel Beach Terrace or the more informal, Beach Terrace Bar.

Getting There

Starting from Mongoose Junction, go east 1.2 miles on Route 20. Turn left on the road leading into the Caneel Bay Resort. Park in the parking lot and take a leisurely walk down the exquisitely landscaped path to the beach.

Be sure to take a stroll through the historic ruins of the estate's old sugar works, which have been tastefully planted and partially restored.

The Caneel Bay resort provides public access to Caneel and Honeymoon Beaches only. Use of the beach chairs, kayaks, sunfish and paddle boats are reserved for registered guests of the hotel.

Facilities

Facilities for day guests include restaurants, public rest rooms and a gift shop.

Snorkeling

Snorkel around the rocks on either side of the bay or explore the sand and grassy center of the bay just off the beach, where you can often find starfish, sea turtles and stingrays.

Caneel Bay

Honeymoon Bay

Salomon Bay

Scott Beach

Caneel Hawksnest

Turtle Bay

Photo by Don Hebert

Caneel Bay History

Over the centuries, Caneel Bay has been occupied by people of diverse cultures and from far away places. From the religious and spiritually oriented culture of indigenous Americans, it passed to the slavery-based plantation system of Europeans and enslaved Africans, then to the subsistence economy of freed slaves and peasant farmers and from there to a series of vacation resorts, starting out as basic cottages and developing into the super-luxurious Caneel Bay Resort of today catering to the well-heeled from North America and beyond.

The first inhabitants of Caneel Bay were the ancestors of the Tainos, who established a village in the coastal section of the valley around 600 AD. For many years, they lived peacefully, planting yucca, fishing, gathering wild fruit, fabricating ceramic pottery, tools and ceremonial objects and conducting their social and religious ceremonies.

This peaceful existence lasted until sometime in the fifteenth century, when the island was reported to be uninhabited.

For the next two centuries, St. John remained only sparsely and intermittently populated by small groups of Native Americans fleeing persecution, pirates, fugitives of all sorts and colors, fishermen and woodcutters. Meanwhile Denmark colonized St. Thomas, and in the early eighteenth century, gave permission to a group of Dutch planters to set up plantations on St. John.

A Dutchman from the island of Statia, Peter Durloe, was one of these original planters. His first claim was what is now called Cinnamon Bay, which he named for the many cinnamon trees, (bay rum) found there. Of course, being Dutch he used the Dutch word for "cinnamon" which is "caneel." Thus, the first Caneel Bay was actually Cinnamon Bay.

What we now call Caneel Bay also had a magnificent stand of bay rum trees for which that bay was similarly named. To distinguish this Caneel Bay from the original Caneel Bay, the former was called Klein Caneel or Little Caneel, and Cinnamon Bay was called Store Caneel or Big Caneel.

When English became the predominant language in the Danish West Indies (now the U.S. Virgin Islands), Store Caneel Bay became know as Cinnamon Bay and Klein Caneel Bay, no longer needing the distinction "little," became know by its present name, Caneel Bay.

In 1733, slaves from the Amina tribe rebelled and took over most of St. John, with the exception of Caneel Bay, where surviving white planters and enslaved Africans from other African tribes with their own long standing animosities against the Aminas, regrouped after the rebellion. With the help of two cannons guarding the entrance to the estate, the small force was able to maintain control of the plantation until the rebellion was put down by French troops from Martinique.

After the rebellion, Caneel Bay continued on as a thriving plantation with sugarcane grown in the mountain valley being refined at the plantation's own sugar works near the beach.

After slavery was abolished, the estate declined and reverted to cattle grazing and subsistence farming, until it was purchased by the West India Company of St. Thomas. Appreciating the natural beauty of the bay, the company began to operate a modest resort building three cottages, a small commissary and a narrow wooden dock. Five additional cottages were gradually constructed by the West India Company. In the

1940s, when the property was acquired by the Trigo brothers from Puerto Rico, four more cottages were built bringing the total to twelve.

The Caneel Bay commissary was described in the 1960 book, *Some True Tales and Legends about Caneel Bay,* by Charlotte Dean Stark:

"In the thirties and forties, the housekeeping cottages were for rent, all except #8, which was the manager's cottage. Everything but food was included - electricity from the Caneel Bay Power Plant, all furnishings, and a St. John maid. Food was bought at the commissary by the maid, or by the lady if she felt like choosing her own groceries. The commissary was described by one visiting cottager as a little country store. Natives from all over the island, as well as the dozen or more cottage guests, bought there, as did the half dozen continental families then living on St. John.

"There would sometimes be as many as twenty-five people all trying to buy at once. That was a crowd in those days."

The Trigo Brothers listed the 500 acre property, along with its seven beautiful beaches and the profitable cottage colony for $75,000. Until Laurence Rockefeller obtained the estate in 1952, rumors abounded as to the ultimate fate of the parcel, some of which were prophetic.

In Desmond Holdridge's 1937 account of life on St. John, *Escape to the Tropics*, he wrote: "Agnes (Agnes Sewer) said that some 'Dane men' had bought Caneel Bay, a beautiful abandoned estate a couple of miles farther west, and were going to run it for tourists.

"'Bout sixty thousand people comin', I expect,' said Agnes, happy thinking of the money, but sad thinking of the strangers and the changes they will make.

"I reassured her. 'Not very many are coming, Agnes. Hjalmar Bang is doing it, and he is just going to build a few houses where white folks that enjoy privacy can live. No hotel, no hot dog stands, no nonsense. It won't change very much.'"

Photo by Don Hebert

41

Photo by Don Hebert

Hawksnest Bay

Why Hawksnest Bay?

Hawksnest Beach is a St. John locals' favorite and the preferred beach for families with children. The reason for this is that Hawksnest is not only one of the most beautiful beaches on St. John, it is also the most convenient. It's the closest north shore beach that you can drive to from Cruz Bay and the parking lot is close to the beach, so there's no need for a long walk carrying your beach accouterments. In the late afternoon, many native St. Johnians come to Hawksnest to "take a soak" after work.

How to Get There

Starting from Mongoose Junction, go 1.8 miles east on route 20. Park in the Hawksnest parking lot.

Facilities

Hawksnest Beach provides ample parking, although on some weekend afternoons, especially when a birthday party or a popular holiday brings more people out, it may be somewhat tight.

The facilities at Hawksnest Beach were upgraded in 2005. There are pit toilets and a changing room, but no running water, thus no showers, sinks or flush toilets.

Between the parking area and the beach is a shady wooded area with two pavilions (covered decks with tables) that are often used for family parties, get-togethers and meetings. These are available on a first come first serve basis after obtaining permission from the National Park (776-6201). Uncovered picnic tables and barbecue grills are also available.

Sunshine

Hawksnest faces east and receives morning sun, so if you enjoy a refreshing swim in the early morning light, Hawksnest is an ideal destination. Conversely, Hawksnest gets shade earlier in the afternoon than other beaches, a plus to some, a minus to others; it's your choice.

Little Hawksnest

Little Hawksnest is a beautiful and almost forgotten stretch of white sandy beach just to the west of Hawksnest Beach. If you want to get away from the crowd to enjoy a little privacy and serenity, Little Hawksnest is an easy two-minute rock scramble to the west or left, if facing the sea.

Little Hawksnest Bay

Caneel Hawksnest Bay

Hawksnest Bay

Hawksnest Bay

Gibney Beach

46

Photo by Don Hebert

Hawksnest Bay

Hawksnest Bay is defined by Hawksnest Point on the west, separating Hawksnest from Caneel Bay and by Perkins Cay on the east, which separates, Hawksnest from Denis Bay. Within the greater bay are four picture-perfect beaches, Caneel Hawksnest, Little Hawksnest, Hawksnest and Gibney.

Photo by Steve Simonsen

The Name

European settlers named the bay, Högsnest. The Geographic Dictionary of the Virgin Islands, written shortly after the United States took control of the territory, explains that this name is probably "compounded from the Danish Hög, meaning Hawk, with Dutch or English Nest." The term "hawk" either referred to the American kestrel, the little hawk that inhabits the island, or to the hawksbill turtle, which used to nest on the sandy shore.

Photo by Gerald Singer

Photo by Don Hebert

50

Snorkeling

It is best to snorkel Hawksnest on days when the bay is calm and there are no north swells to churn up the water and diminish visibility.

The reef that begins just a few yards off the center of the beach is the most popular snorkel at Hawksnest. Snorkel around the perimeter or over the top of the reef where there is sufficient depth. Here you will find several beautiful formations of elegant orange elkhorn corals that look more like small trees than the colonies of animals they actually are.

Hawksnest Bay is home to a wide variety of fish and sea creatures, which seem content to observe you observe them. Have fun!

Beginner Snorkel

To the right facing the water, there is a formation of black rocks that separates Hawksnest Beach from Gibney Beach. Snorkeling around these rocks is an excellent way for beginning snorkelers to practice and gain confidence in a safe, shallow and non-threatening environment while still being able to observe colorful fish, corals and sea creatures. Look for schools of small fish such as grunt, fry and goatfish. Watch the parrotfish grazing the algae and the spunky damselfish defend its territory against all intruders regardless of size.

Photo by Dean Hulse

Gibney Beach

Photo by Gerald Singer

Why Gibney Beach?

There is nothing formal about Gibney Beach. There is no sign, no parking lot and no facilities. It used to be a private beach with no public land access, and although this has recently changed, the beach still retains much of that "private" feeling.

Getting There

Gibney Beach is 0.3 mile east of Hawksnest Beach or 2.1 miles east of Mongoose Junction on Route 20. The entrance to the beach is through the third driveway on your left after passing Hawksnest Beach. Limited parking is available in places where you can pull your vehicle completely off the road. Enter the driveway through the door in the iron gate and walk down the driveway to the shore. The renovated structure at the bottom of the driveway on the right is the former Oppenheimer home, which is now a community center.

The area in front of the community center is sometimes referred to as Oppenheimer Beach, while the longer and wider southwestern part is known as Gibney Beach. They are really the same beach.

Remember that in the Virgin Islands the area from the sea to the line of first vegetation is public domain. Behind the line of first vegetation, though, may be private property, as is the property behind Gibney Beach, which belongs to the Gibney family.

Photo by Don Hebert

Robert and Nancy Gibney and friends enjoy a picnic at Gibney Beach, circa 1950

The Gibneys

In 1946, Robert and Nancy Gibney came to St. John on their honeymoon. The Gibneys were an integral part of the "beat generation," the center of which was New York City's Columbia University. In 1950, the Gibneys bought a forty-acre parcel on Hawksnest Bay and constructed a house just inland from the center of the beach where they lived with their three children.

"Beatniks" evolved to "hippies" and when the Gibney children were teenagers they had many friends among the flower children who would often congregate at Hawksnest. Today the tradition continues, and there is still a definite tendency for Gibney Beach to draw an offbeat crowd.

The Oppenheimers

In 1957, the Gibneys sold a small parcel of their land in Hawksnest to J. Robert Oppenheimer, "the father of the atomic bomb," and his wife, Kitty. The property is at the northeastern extreme of the Gibney's land, where the Oppenheimers built a vacation home on the beach.

Upon the death of J. Robert and later Kitty, Oppenheimer, their daughter Toni inherited the property. When Toni died in 1976, she left it to "the people of St. John" to be used "for a public park and recreation area."

"The people of St. John" proved to be a nebulous entity and, as no provisions were made for maintenance, the house and land fell into disrepair.

Toni's dream was finally realized when the Virgin Islands government took charge of the site and created a community center. Today, for a nominal fee, the center can be rented out for community functions, such as senior citizen outings, Boy Scouts, local reggae and calypso bands, picnics, weddings and birthday parties.

Photo by Don Hebert

Gibney Beach has served as the location for numerous commercials and magazine articles as well as several major motion pictures, including "The Four Seasons" and "Columbus."

Photo by Don Hebert

Photo by Dean Hulse

Snorkeling

Snorkeling is best from the right side or Oppenheimer section of the beach. The entry into the water is over soft sand and the snorkel is suitable for beginners.

Right off the community center (the old Oppenheimer house) is a shallow reef, which occasionally breaks through the surface of the water. Much of this reef was negatively impacted when a heavy rain occurred during the excavation for the Myrah Keating Smith Clinic. Tons of earth were washed down into Hawksnest Bay and the resulting turbidity damaged much of the coral in the bay. Today the reefs are coming back to life and you will see some beautiful live elkhorn and boulder coral, along with fire coral and other examples of reef life. Schools of small fish such as goatfish, grunt and tang can commonly be seen in the area.

A narrow fringing reef runs along the eastern coastline. Close to the beach is a section of beautiful brain coral. The reef here is colorful and there is an abundance of fish. Look for parrotfish, angelfish, squirrelfish, trunkfish and trumpetfish. Also, observe the predators such as yellowtail snapper and blue runners prowling the reef edges on the lookout for fry and other small prey.

More experienced snorkelers can continue along this eastern coast to the point and around to Perkins Cay and Denis Bay. Along the way is a small beach where you can stop and rest. Just before you come to this pocket beach you may see the remains of a sunken sailboat. As you progress northward along the coast you will encounter scattered areas of colorful coral, sponges, fish and other marine life in depths of about six to ten feet. Snorkeling here is best in the summer when there are no ground seas to churn up the water.

Photo by Dean Hulse

Photo by Gerald Singer

Penis Bay

Photo by Don Hebert

Why Denis Bay?

Denis Bay is quiet and secluded, but you will need to be adventurous just to get there, arriving by sea or via a rugged trail though the forest.

Getting There

Look for the narrow path that begins near the bottom of the Peace Hill Trail. The path descends to a secluded section of beach on the western extreme of the bay. The little island just offshore is Perkins Cay.

Denis Bay is now part of the Virgin Islands National Park, but the structures and some of the land behind the beach have been leased to private interests. Please confine your visit to the area between the sea and the line of first vegetation.

Facilities

None

Photo by Steve Simonsen

Photo by Steve Simonsen

Denis Bay History

In the 1920s, Denis bay was acquired by a group of St. Thomas businessmen who operated a club called the Deep Sea Fishing Club, where it was said that "drinking was much more prevalent than fishing." The club was available to the general public with hotel service and conveniences for $22.00 per week with all meals included.

In 1939, Julius and Cleome Wadsworth purchased Denis Bay. Julius was a Foreign Service officer. Cleome was a professional fabric designer and worked in China and in Singapore, where she met Julius. They were married in 1932 and lived in Danszig, Prussia where Julius was serving as Consul. They came to St. John just before the outbreak of World War II in Europe.

The Wadsworths used Denis Bay as a vacation getaway. Their primary home since 1944 had been in Washington DC. Some illustrious St. Johnians have lived at Denis Bay either as renters or caretakers. St. Johnian, Thomas Thomas, served as one of the first caretakers and Robert and Nancy Gibney were among the first renters having leased the property in 1947. The late Carl Frank, the founder of Holiday Homes was also a caretaker. He passed on the enviable job to Peter Griffith and family. One of the Griffith's daughters, Melanie Griffith, who became a famous actress, spent much of her childhood at Denis Bay.

Denis Bay Estate is now the property of the Virgin Islands National Park, although certain "remainder interests", which are the right to use a 1.1 acre parcel, containing the estate house, the warehouse and the old slave quarters will remain in private hands until 2035.

In the 1990s, these "remainder interests" were sold to Ed Fine, son of the "Three Stooges" actor, Larry Fine. These rights have since been resold.

Cleome Wadsworth died on December 28, 1998 at the age of 102. Julius Wadsworth died in April of 1999. He was 96.

Photo by Steve Simonsen

Denis Bay in Days Gone By

The grand staircase was built in Danish times.

The dock at right was destroyed by Hurricane Marilyn in 1995. All that remain today are the pilings.

Snorkeling

The bay is well protected by extensive fringing reefs. From the sea, there is an open channel leading to the center of the beach where there used to be a dock.

When the seas are calm, there is decent snorkeling around the reef especially on its seaward side and around Perkins Cay.

Snorkeling about ten yards offshore of the east side of the remains of the old dock, you can see the coral encrusted fluke of a very large and very old anchor protruding from the sand, pictured on the opposite page.

Photo by Steve Simonsen

Photo by Gerald Singer

Jumbie Bay

Why Jumbie Bay?

If you're looking for a small, private, intimate beach without having to walk a long trail to get there, then Jumbie is an excellent choice.

Getting There

Heading east on the North Shore Road 2.5 miles from Mongoose Junction or 0.2 miles from Peace Hill, is the small parking area on the right side of the road for Jumbie Bay.

Cross the road and walk east about twenty yards to the rustic wooden stairs on your left. At the bottom of the stairs is a short trail leading to the beach.

Sweet Limes

The red berries growing on the thorny dark green shrubs alongside the road and the path to the beach are called sweet limes or limeberries. These edible berries can be eaten as is or made into jams and preserves.

More Privacy and Some Shade

Put your beach blanket down in one of the little coves of sand that extend inland under the small seagrape trees for filtered sunlight and enhanced privacy.

Trade Winds

Jumbie Bay is more exposed to the trade winds than most of the neighboring north shore beaches and the water can get choppy on windy days. On the positive side, the breeze can be refreshing and the rough water can lend a certain drama and intensity to the beach.

Facilities

There are no facilities at this beach other than garbage cans made available and emptied by the National Park Service.

Photo by Steve Simonsen

Photo by Don Hebert

The Name

Jumbie Bay is the only beach on St. John with an African name, coming from the word djambe, and referring to a malevolent supernatural being, similar to the duppy of Jamaica and the zombie of Haiti.

Jumbie Bay is situated in such a way that it cannot readily be seen from passing vehicles on Route 20 or from boats sailing to and from Cruz Bay. Years ago, when there was only a donkey trail on the north shore, Jumbie was even more remote and private than it is today and was reputedly the venue for lovers enjoying private liaisons. Because of this, it was nicknamed Honeymoon Beach. (At that time, Salomon and Honeymoon Beaches did not have separate names, the entire bay being called Salomon.)

Photo by Don Hebert

Photo by Don Hebert

The Far Corner

On the far corner of the beach, there is a beautiful array of dry forest vegetation including two large paddle cacti, a native frangipani and an assortment of wild lilies. There used to be an old stone dock here and a road that led to Denis Bay, which, although overgrown, is still evident.

Photo by Steve Simonsen

Photo by Dean Hulse

Snorkeling

Enter the water in soft sand at either end of the beach.

The center of the bay is sandy. A fringing reef on both sides almost encloses the bay, but is separated by a deep narrow channel marked by buoys.

The top of the reef is shallow and seemingly barren. Under closer observation, you will see an abundance of marine life in the cracks, crevices and holes in the coral. Healthy and colorful hard corals grow on the reef's outer edge.

Snorkeling from this beach is usually best on calm summer days. In the winter, when ground seas are running, or when the seas are rough, there can be waves breaking over the shallow portions of the reef. This stirs up sand and sediment and causes the water to be cloudy.

On calm days, there is good snorkeling around the reefs on both sides of the bay with many examples of healthy, brightly-colored corals, marine invertebrates and colorful tropical fish. Look for parrotfish and schools of blue tang grazing the reef tops.

Beware of shallow areas, and please do not touch or stand on the coral reef.

More advanced snorkelers will enjoy the coral and sponge encrusted rock walls around the headland that separates Jumbie and Denis Bays, which lies to your left looking out towards the sea. Also, just about ten yards offshore of this point, you will find a pie-shaped reef that looks like a multi-colored coral island surrounded on all sides by a sea of sand.

Photo by Don Hebert

Trunk Bay

Photo by Don Hebert

Why Trunk Bay?

Why Trunk? Because it's just so especially beautiful.

Getting There

Trunk Bay is three miles from Mongoose Junction heading east on Route 20. Park in the parking lot and stop at the small building that leads to the beach to pay your entrance fee applicable between 7:30 AM and 4:30 PM. The fees are $4.00 for adults and children younger than 16 enter free. Annual passes are available at $10.00 for an individual and $15.00 for a family. Golden Age and Golden Access National Park Passports are accepted.

The Name

The Geographic Dictionary of the Virgin Islands speculates that the name Trunk Bay "may be from either Trunkscildpatt (the giant leatherback turtle) or Trunkfish." My choice would be that of the impressive leatherback, which can be as much as nine feet long and weigh over 2,000 pounds.

Facilities

Showers, bathrooms and changing areas are available between 7:30 AM and 4:30 PM.

Also available are public telephones, picnic tables, barbecue grills and a covered pavilion. (To reserve the covered pavilion for a private event, call the National Park at 776-6201.)

A gift shop provides just about everything you might need while at the beach, such as sun screen, towels, insect repellent, hats, tee-shirts, bathing suits, film, batteries, books, post cards and souvenirs. Lockers, snorkel equipment, flotation devices and beach chairs are available for rent. The gift shop is open from 9:00 AM to 3:30 PM. Rental equipment must be returned by 3:00 PM.

The snack bar is open between 9:00 AM and 4:30 PM.

The organization, Friends of the Park, operate a kiosk staffed by volunteers where you can by books and other park related material. It has been described by one Park Ranger as "a miniature Visitors Center."

Jumbie Bay

Denis Bay

Underwater Trail

Trunk Cay

Photo by Don Hebert

Brief History of Trunk Bay

The Amerindian inhabitants of St. John, known as the Tainos, established a village at Trunk Bay around 700 AD, which lasted until about 900 AD, when they apparently left in a hurry, evidenced by the archeological find of abandoned cooking pots still filled with food.

In colonial times, Trunk Bay was operated as a sugar estate and prospered until shortly after the emancipation of the slaves, when the entire island underwent a period of economic decline.

In the late 1920s Paul Boulon Sr. used to visit St. John from his home in Puerto Rico. While there he often spent time at the Fishing Club at Denis Bay, which is described by Desmond Holdbridge in his book *Escape to the Tropics*, written in 1937 as "a quaint institution, now non-existent, where no fishing was ever done." It was during a Fishing Club get-together that he learned that Trunk Bay and 100 additional acres of land were for sale for $2500.

Paul and his wife, Erva bought the property and built a house on the hill overlooking the eastern end of the beach where they and their four children would spend their summer vacations there. One of the family's favorite activities was to explore the bay and the little caves around Trunk Cay in their genuine "Old Town" canoe that they had specially sent down from Maine.

The house went unoccupied for several years around the time of World War II. In 1947, Mrs. Boulon and her son Paul returned to St. John, fixed up the house and opened a small hotel that attracted the more adventurous New York literati, journalists, psychoanalysts, theater people and even vacationing FBI agents.

The actors, Richard Widmark and Henry Fonda, and the nuclear scientist, J. Robert Oppenheimer, were frequent guests.

John Dos Pasos, whose books include, *Manhattan Transfer, USA Trilogy, Adventures of a Young Man* and *Orient Express*, met and wooed his wife at the Boulon's guest house, on Trunk Bay, an appropriate venue for this famous author who once summed up his life's works as "man's struggle for life against the strangling institutions he himself creates."

John Gunther, author of such works as *Inside Europe, Inside Asia, Inside Latin America, Inside U.S.A., Inside Africa, Inside Russia, Inside Europe, Inside South America,* and *Inside Australia* also vacationed with the Boulons at Trunk Bay. As there was no good road to Trunk Bay at the time, he arrived by sea and came ashore in a dinghy along with his entourage and his luggage. When the dinghy reached the beach, the Boulon's hotel staff offloaded the luggage and helped the dinghy passengers ashore. Gunther insisted on personally carrying his briefcase, which contained the notes for his work *Inside Africa*. As he was exiting the craft, he fell into the water causing someone to remark that "Trunk Bay is now Inside Gunther."

In 1958, The Boulons sold Trunk Bay to Laurance Rockefeller, with the exception of their houses and property on the hillside and small beach on the eastern headland of the bay. Rockefeller then donated this land and most of his other St. John holdings to the National Park. During the ten years that the Boulons operated their quaint pension at Trunk Bay, it was said there were rarely more than five or six people on the beach.

Photo by Don Hebert

Sunset Weddings

Trunk Bay has become a popular venue for couples seeking a romantic tropical location for their wedding vows.

Avoiding the Crowd

Trunk Bay receives as many as 1,000 visitors per day including locals, cruise ship passengers, party boats, and tourists from the island's villas and hotels.

Nonetheless, you can still enjoy Trunk Bay in its pristine state as long as you can do without amenities such as life guards, snack bars, shops and showers. All you have to do is arrive early in the morning or late in the afternoon.

Photo by Steve Simonsen

Snorkeling

Trunk Bay is the home of the National Park's underwater snorkeling trail. It begins just offshore of the spit of land that juts out toward Trunk Cay and is marked by buoys.

The trail consists of a series of underwater monuments with signs providing environmental information and identifying some of the flora and fauna common to the coral reef.

Fish survey volunteers report that on the average you should see (if not identify) 30 distinct species of fish in a half hour snorkel of the Trunk Bay Underwater Trail.

An Experiment

Coral colony fragments transplanted onto this reef may be used to accelerate recovery of damaged reefs elsewhere.

Photo by Steve Simonsen

Cinnamon Bay

Why Cinnamon Bay?

Cinnamon is the place to go for beach activities and water sports. Besides the regular swimming, sunning, snorkeling and picnicking, Cinnamon offers windsurfing, kayaking, volleyball, and camping.

Getting There

Cinnamon Bay is 3.9 miles east of Mongoose Junction on Route 20. Park in the parking lot and walk to the beach, which is about a quarter mile away over a flat, shady paved track.

For those without vehicles, there is a scheduled taxi service between Cruz Bay and Trunk Bay.

Facilities

Cinnamon Bay is operated as a campground and offers facilities designed to support the campers staying there. These facilities are also available to the public. They include a small general store carrying basic provisions, the T'ree Lizards restaurant, a snack bar, lockers, rest rooms, changing rooms, showers, telephones, picnic tables and barbecue grills.

An activities desk offers snorkel trips, SCUBA, snorkel and windsurfing lessons, day sails, cocktail cruises and National Park activities such as the Reef Bay Hike and the Waters Edge Walk.

Entrances to the Cinnamon Bay Loop Trail and the Cinnamon Bay Trail are located across the road from the main parking lot.

At the end of the road to the beach on your left (west), you will find Cinnamon Bay Watersports where you can rent sea and surfing kayaks, beach floats, windsurfers and sailboats. Cinnamon Bay Watersports also offers windsurfing and sailing lessons.

On the east side of the track is an old historic Danish building, which houses the temporary archeological museum in the western part of the building and the Beach Shop on the eastern side, which offers swimsuits, toys, souvenirs, snacks and drinks as well as snorkeling equipment and beach chair rentals.

The temporary museum features Taino and plantation day artifacts found at the Cinnamon Bay archeological dig. The excavation site is just east of the museum on the inland side of the dirt road.

Surfing

Cinnamon is the only beach on St. John where surfers and experienced boogie boarders can take advantage of the north swell that comes in the winter.

Photo by Don Hebert

Photo by Steve Simonsen

Windsurfing

Cinnamon Bay offers the best windsurfing on St. John. The winds are relatively calm near shore, which is good for beginners. As you go offshore, however, more advanced windsurfers will find strong, steady winds, but without the waves that are usually associated with forceful wind conditions.

Photo by Don Hebert

Little Cinnamon

Want some seclusion? Try Little Cinnamon Bay.

To get there, walk along the beach to your left (west) and continue on to the end of the sandy beach. Take the narrow trail that leads through the bush along the shoreline and over a section of rocks, before emerging at the beach at Little Cinnamon.

Photo by Don Hebert

Snorkeling

Beginning snorkelers can explore the area around the rocks at the eastern end of the beach or between Cinnamon and Little Cinnamon Bay. It's an easy snorkel on calm days and there's a lot to see.

Going a little further out, there is very good snorkeling around Cinnamon Cay, the little island just offshore from the beach.

At Little Cinnamon, snorkelers may find the remains of an old Cessna aircraft that crashed and sank years ago. The propeller, the engine and one of the wings are visible most of the year. The wreck is in shallow water and can be found by snorkeling out from the eastern portion of the beach between the old stone wall and the first set of coconut palms.

Photo by Don Hebert

Maho Bay

Why Maho Bay?

Maho is the only north shore beach that you can drive right up to. It's the very informality of this beautiful and often-photographed beach that makes it so special. It's right there by the side of the road, no parking lots or signs, just the beach. Stately groves of coconut palms line both sides of the road. Just pull over under a maho tree and there you are!

In addition to its convenience, Maho Bay is calm and shallow, making it a great place to bring the kids, get them used to the water or teach them how to swim.

Getting There

Maho Bay is located about 1.25 miles past Cinnamon Bay or 5.2 miles past Mongoose Junction going east on Route 20. Park off the side of the road.

Facilities

On the western part of the beach is a National Park pavilion on the extreme western portion of the beach. A permit must be obtained from the park in order to use this facility. This permit will also entitle you to use the bathrooms to the west of the pavilion, which are otherwise locked and not available to the general public. The park will explain the rules and conditions pertaining to the use of the pavilion. (Call the National Park at 776-6201)

The Goat Trail leading to the Maho Bay Campground at Little Maho Bay can be found at the eastern end of the beach where the road turns inland.

Photo by Don Hebert

Photo by Steve Simonsen

Maho Bay was named after the Hibiscus tilaceus or beach maho, a tree commonly found on the St. John shoreline and throughout the tropics. The beach maho has a distinctive heart shaped leaf and produces attractive yellow flowers that later turn purple. The small green fruit of the maho is not edible, but a bush tea can be made from the leaf.

Photo by Gerald Singer

Snorkeling

The warm, calm, shallow waters of Maho Bay make it an excellent place to teach children how to swim or snorkel.

There is good snorkeling along the rocky shorelines on both sides of the bay, as well as over the grass beds in the center where you may find sea turtles, conch and sting rays.

Photo by Steve Simonsen

Photo by Don Hebert

Francis Bay

Why Francis Bay?

Francis Bay is a beach that really invites you to settle down and stay a while. It's an ideal beach for a picnic. The bay faces west, leeward of the trade winds and tends to be calmer than other north shore beaches.

During the week, there are not many visitors here, and because the beach is so big, it is almost always possible to find a nice private spot.

Getting There

If you are coming from Cruz Bay via Route 20, proceed to Maho Bay where the road leaves the shoreline and turns inland towards the right. From here, continue about 1.5 miles where you will come to an intersection with the road that runs along the Leinster Bay shoreline. Turn left and go to the stone building, which will be on your right. You can park here and take the walking trail or continue straight to the end of the road where you can park near the beach.

If you are arriving from Cruz Bay via Centerline Road, turn left at the Colombo Yogurt stand. Go down the hill and turn right at the first intersection. This will take you to the Leinster Bay shoreline where you will turn left and proceed to either the parking area by the stone building and take the walking trail or directly to the parking area by the beach.

Facilities

Portable toilets are located at the main parking area where there is also a dumpster for trash. Picnic tables and barbecues can be found nestled between the trees at the edge of the beach.

Photo by Don Hebert

Photo by Don Hebert

Photo by Steve Simonsen

The Francis Bay Trail runs along the salt pond located just inland of the beach and is an excellent place for bird watching, especially early in the morning

Photo by Steve Simonsen

Photo by Dean Hulse

Snorkeling

The rocky north coast on the right hand side of the beach offers excellent snorkeling, especially during the summer months when large schools of fry congregate close to shore. These small silvery fish travel in close proximity to one another in large schools that look like moving underwater shadows.

On the outskirts of these living clouds, in slightly deeper water, lurk predators, such as jacks, yellowtail snapper, Spanish mackerel and barracuda as well some respectfully-sized tarpon and pompano. Every now and then, one of these larger fish will enter to feed, moving quickly into the glittery mass. The fry are extremely sensitive to minute changes in water currents and can sense the approach of the hunters. In a burst of speed, they move away from the oncoming predators. Some are successful and some are eaten. Some breach the surface of the water, fly through the air and splash back into the sea. This splash, however, puts them into yet more danger. Waiting pelicans and brown boobies swoop down in the vicinity of the splash scooping up big mouthfuls of unlucky fry.

In the midst of all this activity, large schools of French grunts, oblivious to the drama around them, hover, almost motionless, over and around colorful live coral. Parrotfish and blue tang swim about grazing on algae. Little damselfish defend their self-proclaimed territories by darting menacingly at even large intruders.

A closer look will reveal all sorts of beautiful and mysterious sea creatures like small eels, feather duster and Christmas tree worms, brightly colored sponges and gracefully swaying gorgonians such as the colorful sea fan.

In the underwater grasslands just seaward of the reef, snorkelers are likely to come upon large green sea turtles often accompanied by stuck-on remora or bar jacks that follow along just inches above the turtle's back. In this area one may also see southern stingrays, conch, trunkfish, and others.

Novices who feel more comfortable close to shore can have a rewarding snorkel around the rocks on the south side of the bay between Francis and little Maho or over the seagrass that lies in shallow water on the other end of the beach.

Photo by Don Hebert

Leinster Bay

Photo by Steve Simonsen

Why Leinster Bay?

Getting There

To reach Leinster Bay, follow the directions to Francis Bay, but turn right, instead of left, when you get to the water's edge. Go about a quarter mile to the end of the paved road where you'll find the parking lot for the Annaberg Sugar Mill. Park your vehicle and walk down the Leinster Bay Trail, the dirt track that follows the coastline.

Leinster Bay Trail

The distance from the parking lot to the beach is a little over three quarters of a mile.

The Leinster Bay Trail is a particularly beautiful walk. It goes right along the water's edge providing splendid, unobstructed views of Leinster Bay, the Narrows and the Sir Francis Drake Channel.

Facilities

There are pit toilets and a trash bin near the parking lot.

Leinster
Bay Trail

Photo by Steve Simonsen

Historical Note

Because dueling was illegal in the Danish West Indies, those convinced of the necessity of settling disputes or defending their honor in this manner would travel to Tortola where the practice was legal. In 1800, however, the British Virgin Islands also prohibited dueling.

Consequently, the remote and uninhabited island of Waterlemon Cay, far from the eyes of Danish or British authorities, became the new "field of honor."

Snorkeling

From the beach, you can access the fine snorkeling around Waterlemon Cay, the small island just offshore. (Many visitors name this as their favorite snorkel.)

Enter the water from the beach and snorkel to the island. The shoreline water is shallow, and the bottom is a mixture of sand and coral rubble. It is about a 0.2-mile snorkel to the fringing reef off Waterlemon Cay. Between the beach and the island you will snorkel over an environment of seagrass in about twenty feet of water where you can often see starfish, green turtles and stingrays.

To decrease the snorkeling distance to the island, follow the trail at the far end of the beach. Bear left at the first fork in the trail, which runs along the coastline. At the end of this trail, walk along the shore and choose a convenient place close to Waterlemon Cay to enter the water. The distance across the channel to the island is only about 0.1 mile. This entry is from the rocky shoreline to a rocky bottom. Be careful not to step on live coral or sea urchins.

Photo by Don Hebert

From this entry point to the eastern part of Waterlemon Cay, you will snorkel over an area of seagrass and scattered reef. Closer to the island, the water becomes quite shallow. Here you will see schools of blue tang and some very large parrotfish. You can sometimes hear the parrotfish crunching their beak-like teeth along the surface of the rocks and dead coral.

The south and east sides of Waterlemon Cay are bordered by a shallow-water fringing reef. The reef on the west and north sides of the cay is deeper, descending to a depth of about twenty feet. The reef is teeming with fish and other sea creatures. There are several varieties of coral to be found here, all healthy and colorful and the sea fans and sea plumes found in the deeper parts of the reef will give you the impression of swimming about in an underwater forest.

Look for eels in holes in the reef and for octopus where you find opened seashells piled together.

Caution
There is often an offshore current around Waterlemon Cay, especially on the western side of the island, which will be stronger during new and full moons. If you are not a strong swimmer, keep this in mind. If you get into trouble, follow the current; go around the island and return on the other side.

Photo by Don Hebert

Photo by Dean Hulse

Salt Pond Bay

Why Salt Pond Bay?

Salt Pond Bay is a conveniently-located white sand beach for those residing in, or visiting the Coral Bay side of the island. It is also an excellent alternative for those seeking calm water on days when the surf is breaking on the north.

Getting There

To reach Salt Pond Bay take route 107 heading south for 3.9 miles starting from the Moravian Church in Coral Bay. The quarter mile trail to the beach begins at the parking area.

Facilities

Facilities include chemical toilets, picnic tables and barbecues.

Snorkeling

The best snorkeling is along the rocky eastern coastline.

Photo by Don Hebert

Trails

Two National Park trails can be accessed from the far (south) end of the beach.

The quarter mile Drunk Bay Trail passes by a salt pond, where salt can be harvested during periods of dry weather, usually around June and July. The trail continues on to the rocky and windswept beach at Drunk Bay, an excellent beach for beach combing, but too rough and dangerous for swimming.

The Ram Head Trail is about a mile long and leads to Ram Head Point, which is two hundred feet above sea level with sheer rocky cliffs descending to the Caribbean where you can enjoy the dramatic and spectacular view.

The National Park recommends extra water and a hat due to the particularly hot and sunny condition of the area, along with the fact that you will eventually have to make the quarter mile uphill trek back to the parking lot.

Photo by Don Hebert

Legend of Ram Head

Old legends say Ram Head is a special and magical wishing point. Throw a rock from the top of the cliff and shout out a wish as loud as you can while your rock is in the air. If you finish shouting your wish before the rock hits the water, and if your rock hits the water without hitting the cliff or other rocks, your wish will come true. The rules for wishing as outlined by the genie in the movie "Aladdin" apply. This means no wishing for more wishes, wishing for people to fall in love, etc. Personal experience has shown that this legend is real, and a well-thrown rock, coupled with a fast, loud, wish, will make a wish come true.

Lameshur Bay

Photo by Gerald Singer

Why Lameshur Bay?

Like Salt Pond, Lameshur is an excellent alternative to north shore beaches, especially on days when winter swells may make swimming and snorkeling on the north uncomfortable. Lameshur is further away and harder to drive to than Salt Pond, involving a difficult and steep section of road, but unlike Salt Pond, the beach is conveniently located right next to the parking area.

Lameshur is also a perfect place to take a refreshing dip in the sea after exploring the nearby ruins or taking a hike on the Lameshur Bay or Bordeaux Mountain Trails.

Getting There

At the end of route 107 traveling south continue one mile on the dirt road. This road becomes very steep and rutted. A four-wheel drive vehicle and off-road driving experience may be necessary. As a matter of fact, most rental car agencies have declared this section of road "off limits." You can park anywhere along the road in the vicinity of the beach.

Facilities

Facilities include picnic tables, barbecues and chemical toilets

Photo by Don Hebert

Snorkeling

The best snorkeling is along the coast on the eastern side of the bay and around the rocks just off the beach in calm shallow water.

Photo by Steve Simonsen

Photo by Steve Simonsen